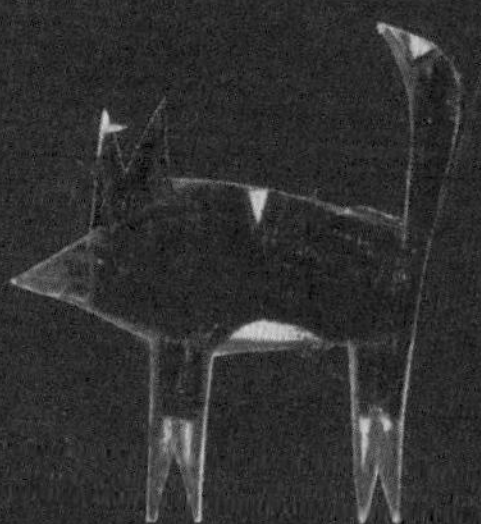

23
24
26
25
14
15
02
12
11

For my family

Dion

To Joie Boulter, whose humour, resilience and ginger nut biscuits are the glue in this story

Johanna

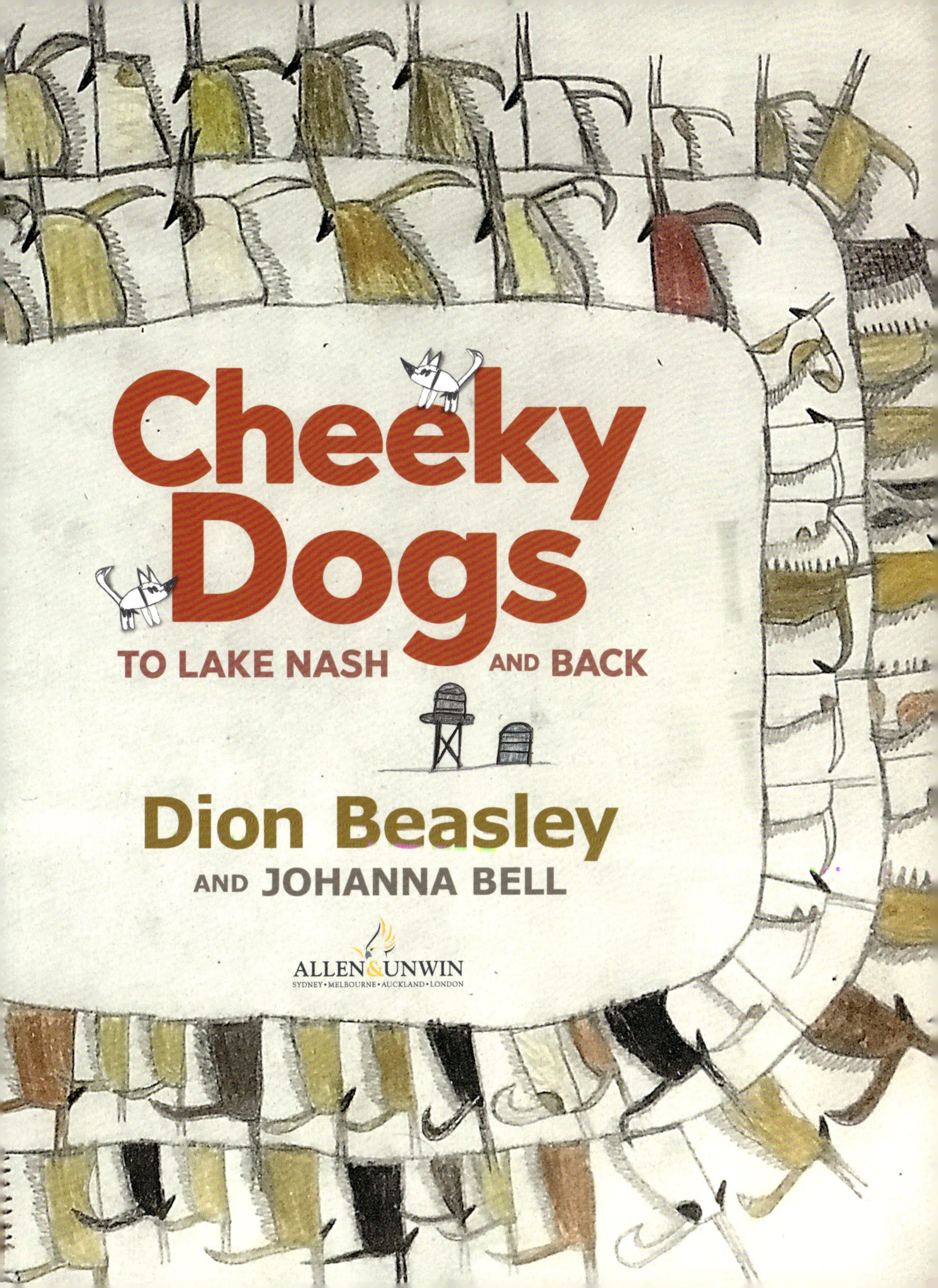

Cheeky Dogs

TO LAKE NASH AND BACK

Dion Beasley

AND JOHANNA BELL

ALLEN&UNWIN

SYDNEY • MELBOURNE • AUCKLAND • LONDON

The development of *Cheeky Dogs: To Lake Nash and Back* was proudly sponsored by the Northern Territory Government.

Proudly sponsored by NORTHERN TERRITORY GOVERNMENT

First published by Allen & Unwin in 2019

Allen & Unwin
83 Alexander Street
Crows Nest NSW 2065
Australia
Phone: (61 2) 8425 0100
Email: info@allenandunwin.com
Web: www.allenandunwin.com

A Cataloguing-in-Publication entry is available from the National Library of Australia
www.trove.nla.gov.au

ISBN 978 1 76052 811 9

For teaching resources, explore
www.allenandunwin.com/resources/for-teachers

Cover design and text design by Ruth Grüner
Typesetting by Ruth Grüner
Set in 12pt Sabon by Ruth Grüner

Printed in February 2019 by C&C Offset Printing Co. Ltd, China

1 3 5 7 9 10 8 6 4 2

MIX
Paper from responsible sources
FSC® C008047
FSC www.fsc.org

My family and Aboriginal and
Torres Strait Islander people are advised that
this book contains the names and pictures
of people who have passed away.
D.B.

8
9
10
11
12
13
14
15
16
17
18
19
20
21

23
24
25
26
27
28
29
30
31
32
33
34
35

Alice Springs. 1991.
My mum came in on the back road from Lake Nash.
Rough, rough, bumpy, bumpy.
Me in her belly.

After I was born, she took the same road back.
Straight past Utopia, all the way to Lake Nash.
We stayed there for a bit.
What colour house? I don't know.
How many dogs? I don't know.

Then I was in Elliott with my aunty
and her mother and their kids
and a little black dog. **Shut the gate!**
Aunty says the house was made of grey bricks.

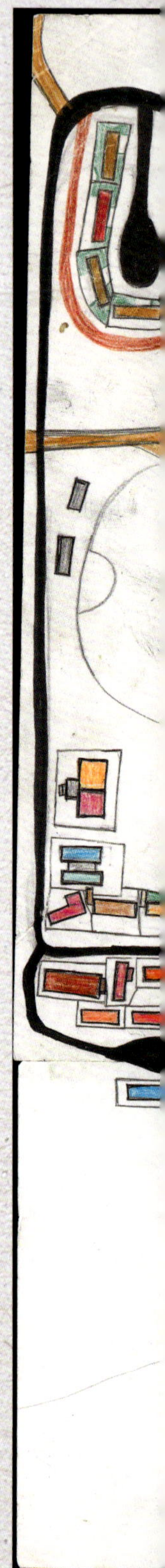

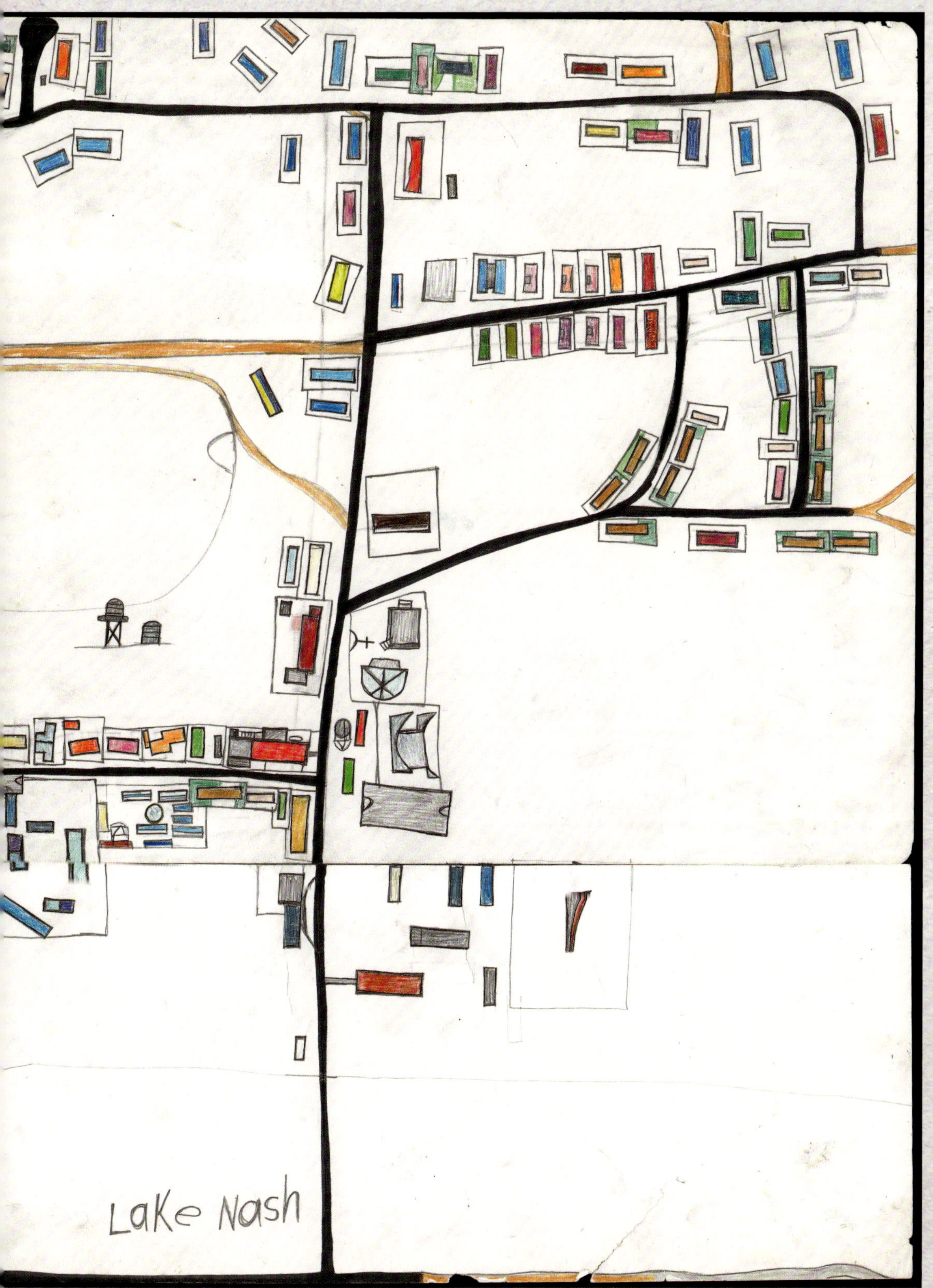
Lake Nash

Next stop – Mount Isa. Upstairs house.
Lots and lots of stairs but no dogs.

Lake Nash.
Elliott.
Lake Nash.
Soapy Bore.
Lake Nash.
Ampilatwatja.
Back to Lake Nash.

Everywhere the earth was red.

Plenty, plenty dogs.

My dad would drive us in his yellow car.
Rough, rough, bumpy, bumpy
all the way to Canteen Creek.

Lake Nash again, my mother's place.
All of us in a brown house and
a blue house too. All of us together –
Mum, Dad, me and my sister
standing in the doorway with her thumbs
sticking up. Tall trees out the back.
Two small and two big beautiful trees.

Cooking outside.
Eating damper with strawberry jam.
Dad turning kangaroo in the coals.
How did he catch that kangaroo?
Gun? No.   Spear? No.
A brown dog in the grass
chasing, chasing.
Teeth in the meat
straight on the fire.

Six big dogs sitting in a circle.
One black, one white.
One brown with stripes.
One grey with his tail chopped off.
One father dog with lots of spots
and an old dog with white whiskers.

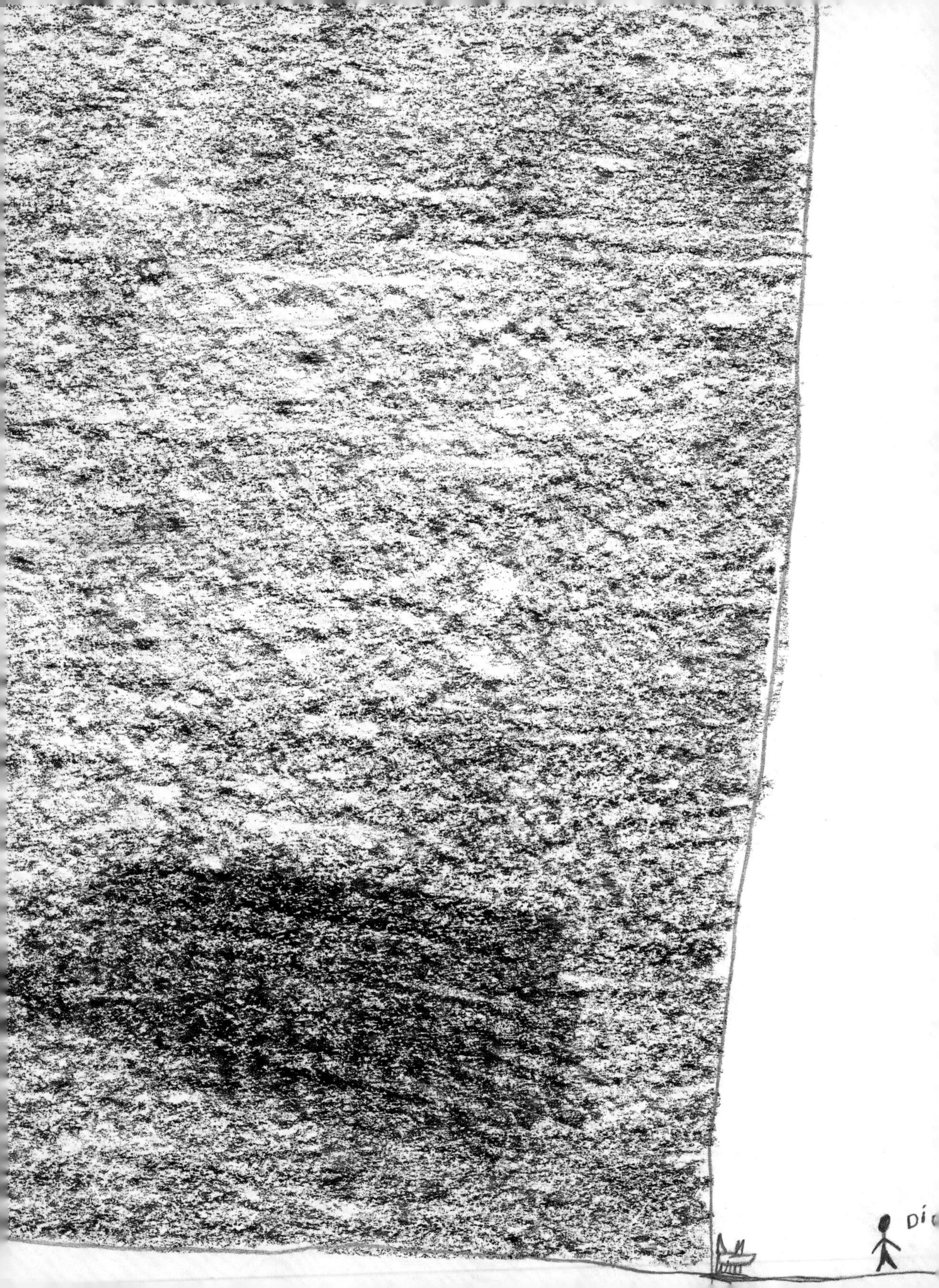

My legs
worked
back then.
Walking
walking
everywhere.
Strong feet.
No shoes.

My grandmother tells a story about
when I was small, four, maybe five.
My dad gone somewhere and me
looking, looking.
Out of the house, down the road
walking, walking.
Hot sun, dry mouth
tired, tired.
They found me where the bullocky drink
a long, long way from home.

I'm three, maybe four.

I walk to the shop

to buy flour.

Three big angry dogs

are following me.

Hair up.
Sharp teeth.
I am screaming
SCARED.
Looking, looking
for somewhere
to hide.

The sign outside

the shop says

NO DOGS ALLOWED!

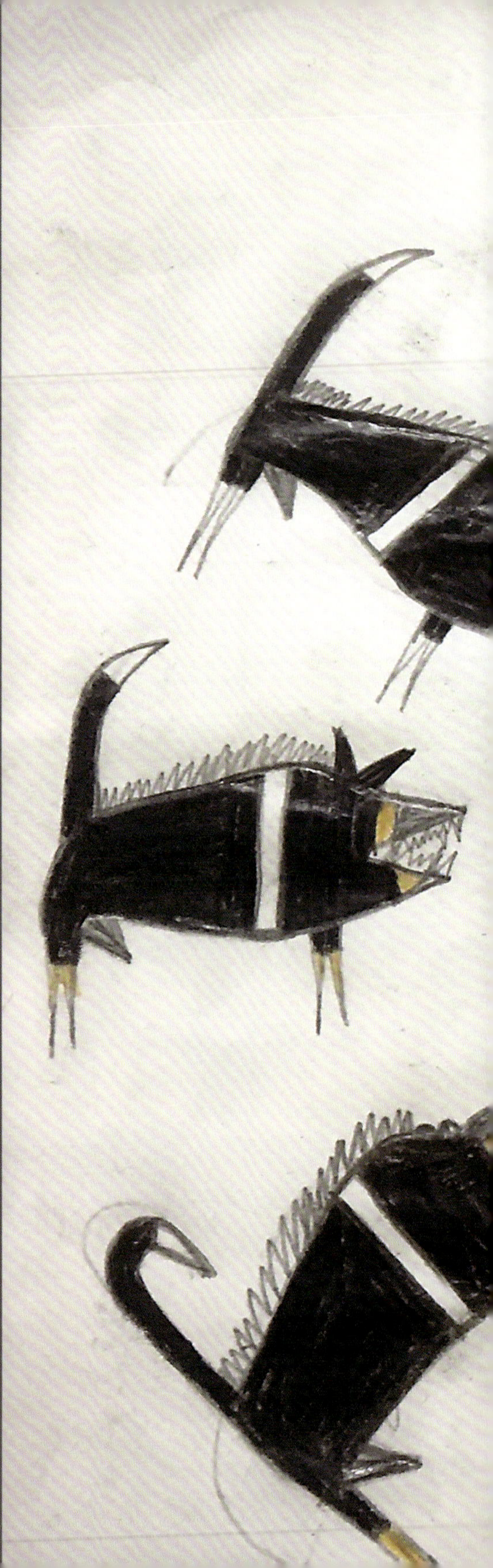

I am running, running running for the shop.

A man picks me up
and takes me to the clinic.

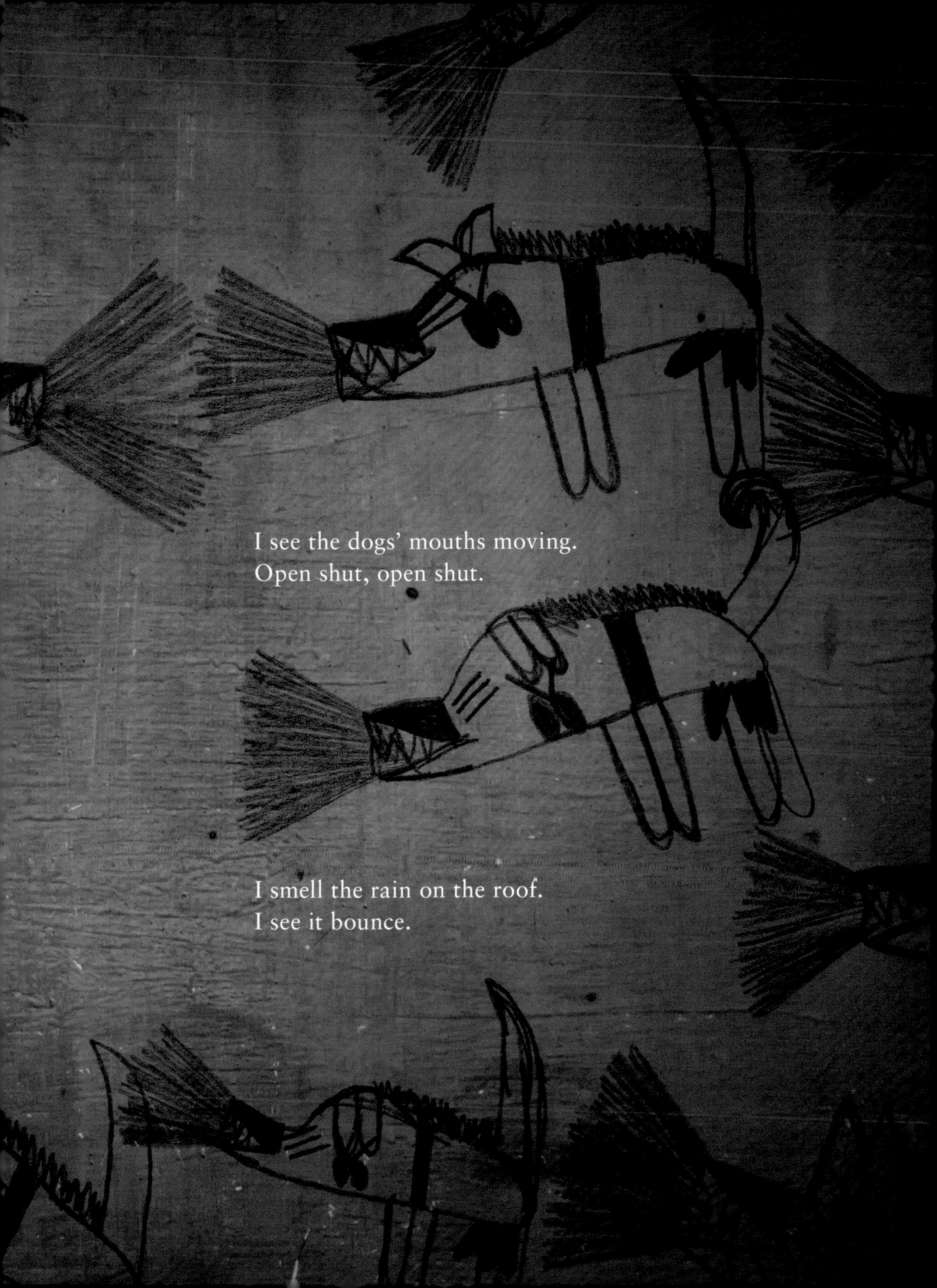

I see the dogs' mouths moving.
Open shut, open shut.

I smell the rain on the roof.
I see it bounce.

My mum is a Morton and my dad is a Beasley
but now I live with the Boulters –
Tony and Joie.
Our house is on Fazaldeen Road.
Drive south. Turn right. Go straight.
If you get to the dump you've gone too far.

I used to live with my grandad
at number six Mulga Camp.
He was a Beasley too.
I loved him very much
but now he's gone.

He always wore a hat
and his beard was white and prickly
same like dry grass.

We used to sit outside and count the dogs.

Two brown father dogs
three black brother dogs
and one small mother dog
who liked to fight.

Grandad's house
No. 6.
5
Mulga
Wuppa
Sport + Rec
4
cycle
Peko
Park
swimming
Pool
Race Track
1
yinkKa
Nyunyu
church
Battery
Hill
3
ence
Karguru

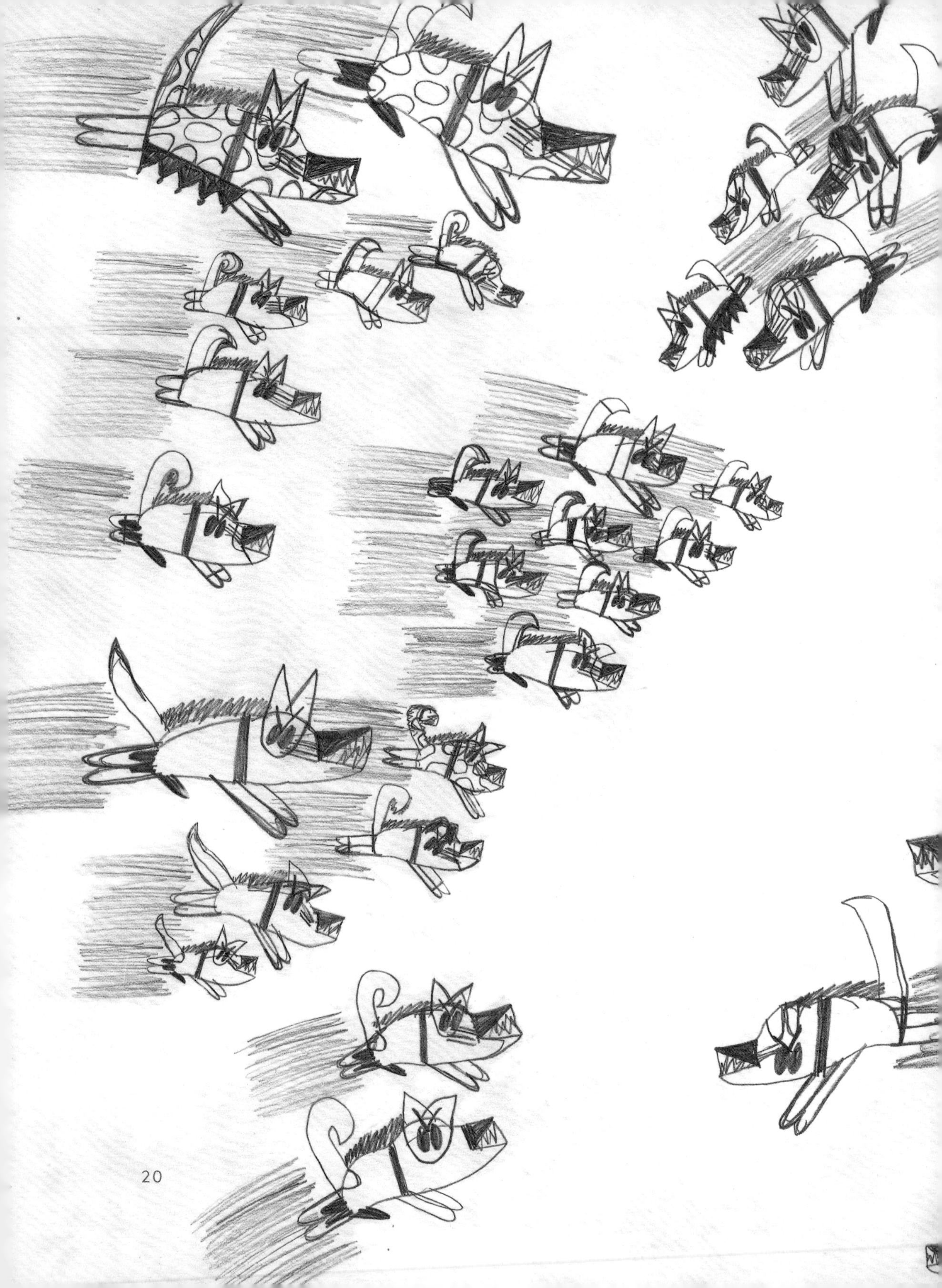

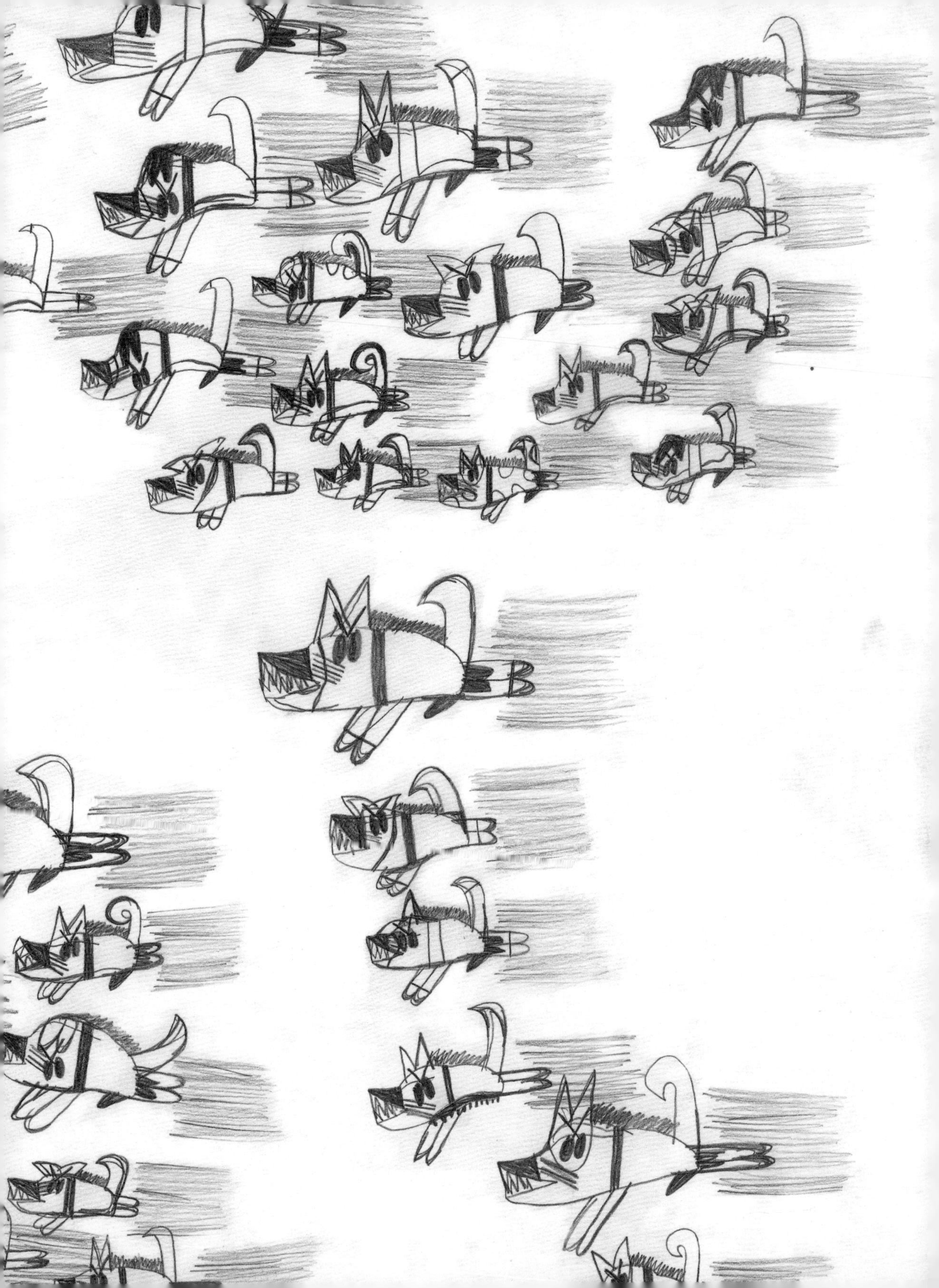

When Grandad got sick,
he called Joie over.
Dion can come live with you
up on Fazaldeen Road.
Tony looked worried but Joie said yes.
Happy, happy she was
and me too.

1
19
20
2
23
25

DARWIN
ARAFURA SEA
ARNHEM
LAND
GULF
OF

I draw Joie, thin like a stick with glasses.
She is always busy, busy
making, making
T-shirts and bags and biscuits and stew.
Not pork! Just beef.
That's what I like
and sausages too, every morning
spitting in the pan.

Tony has a big stomach
and bright blue eyes.
He likes collecting stamps and playing tricks.
It's just us three.
No dogs.

I want to get one
but first, we need a fence!

All the dogs are down
at Mulga Camp
Wuppa Camp
Tingkkarli
Karguru
Village Camp
Dump Camp
and Blueberry Hill.
Plenty, plenty dogs in Tennant Creek.

I ride down to feed them
on my favourite scooter.
Chicken necks and chopped up bones.
That's what they like best.
Chuck the meat and watch the dogs
come running.

Big ones, little ones, black ones, brown.

Ears pointing up and ears flopping down.

Short tails, long tails, brown stripes, white.

Too many cheeky dogs.
Too many fights.

Once, at Grandad's house, there was a very big fight.
Plenty, plenty dogs
chasing, chasing, barking, barking.
Hair up, teeth out, ears ripped.
Dust flying into the sky.
The air was brown and the ground was red.

The next morning the black mother dog was dead.
Her body went hard like a rock.
Then it blew up
same like the balloons
at the Tennant Creek show.
We buried her in the ground
out the back of Grandad's house.

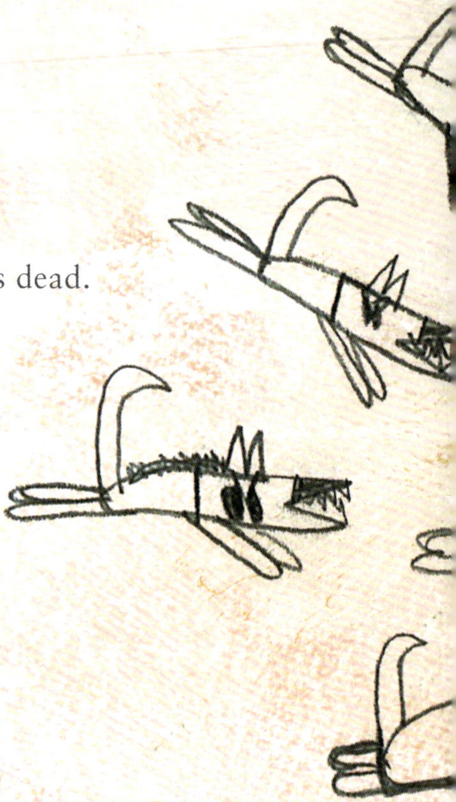

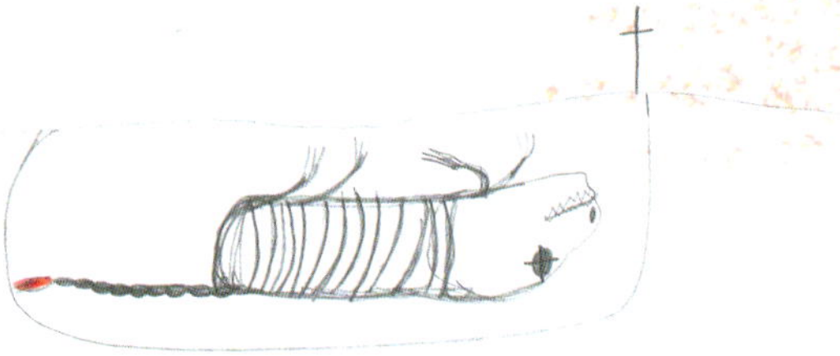

My favourite dogs at Mulga Camp are
Trouble, Bessie and Ralph.
Trouble is tall with ears sticking up.
Bessie is short with belly near the ground.
Ralph lives at number eleven.
He's all brown with a blue collar.

I feed them every day.
I feed them when the sun is hot
and after the storms make everything mud.
I feed them when they are sick
and when the yard is full of pups.
Now only Ralph is left.
He's old and his ear is ripped.
He better watch out or the other dogs
will get him.

The dogcatcher nearly got him once.
He came around with his stick
and his truck
and took all the bad dogs away.
Where did they go? I don't know.

6
18
7
21
4
22
15
25
24
23
14
26

Maybe he took them to Canteen Creek.

When the vets come to Tennant Creek they let me watch.
The dogs look dead but they're not. ***Just sleeping.***
They cut them open and sew them back up.
When they wake, their legs are wobbly.
Stumble trip. Stumble trip.
Sometimes they crawl
like me.

The vet gives them stitches and brown medicine.
Don't worry Joie says. ***The stitches will fall out***
and just a scar will be left.
Like the scar on my stomach
hard like a stone.
Teeth in my skin
a long time ago.

Mulga

6
18
7
15
25
24

At home with Joie and Tony
I make families of dogs.
Black brother dogs
white mother dogs
brown ones with stripes and spots.
Running. Sitting. Lying down.

I draw the dogs and cut them out.
I roll them from paper and foil
or pieces of bread.
Whatever I can find.
I turn the floor into a giant camp for dogs.
I use paper and grass and rocks.

Some are small like pebbles.
Others as big as my head.
Some stay here and some go away
on buses and planes
to Melbourne, Darwin, Hervey Bay
and the MCA in Sydney.

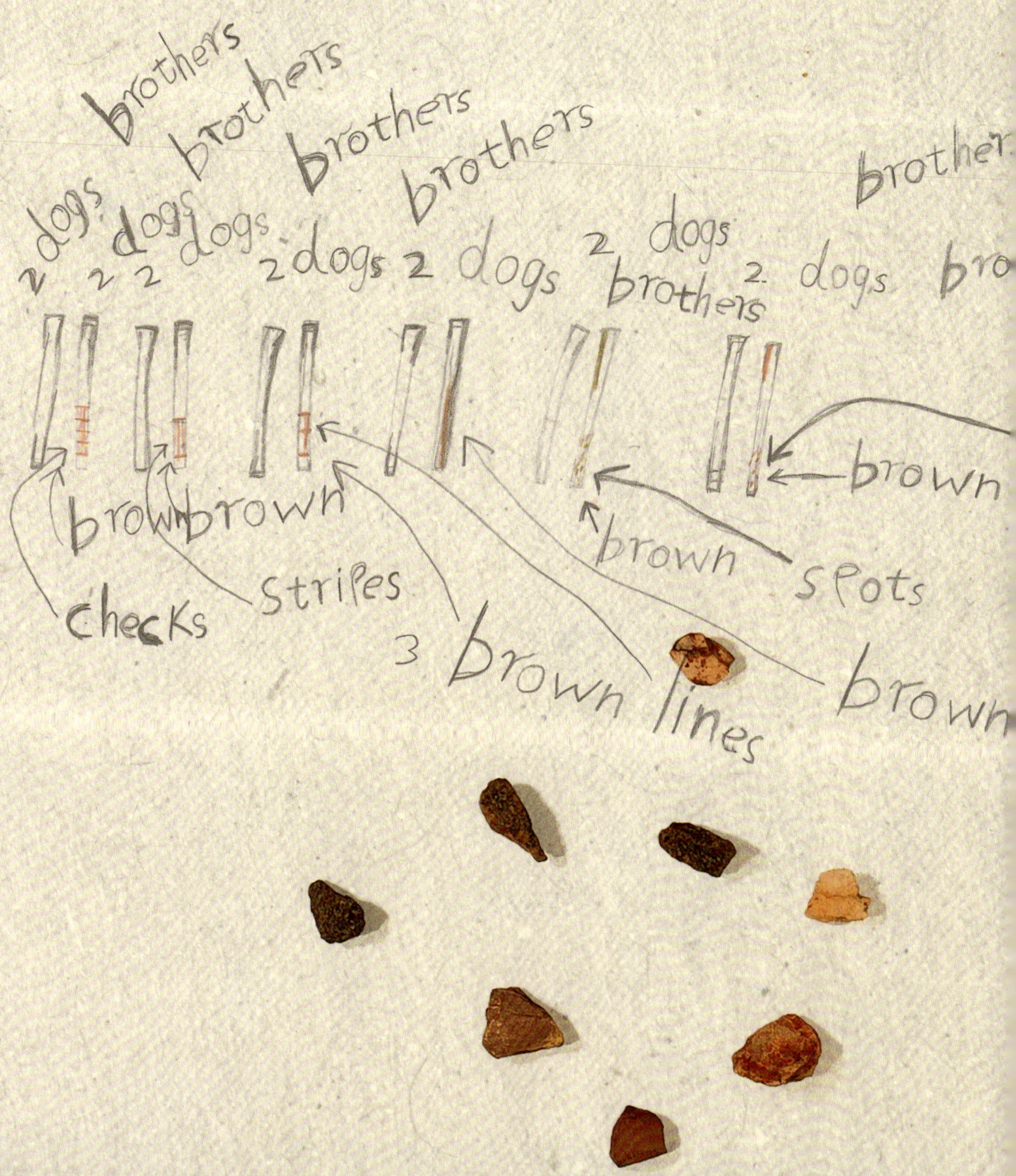
brothers
2 dogs
brothers
2 dogs
brothers
2 dogs
brothers
2 dogs
brothers
2 dogs
2 dogs
brothers
2 dogs
brother
bro
brown
brown
checks
stripes
3 brown lines
brown
spots
brown
brown

cheekydogs

I go too.
Down to Alice Springs then up, up into the sky.
In Sydney the buildings are tall.
I look for dogs but there are none.
Just lots of people walking fast and seagulls stealing chips.
I want to feed the dogs at Mulga Camp but it's too far.
Joie takes me to the park to feed the ducks instead.
I count down the days.
Four sleeps.
Three.
Two.
One.
Home.
Hop into bed.
I love Tennant Creek.

Me in my room.
My dogs spreading out.
Messy, messy, fighting on the floor.
Big ones, little ones, black ones, brown.
Ears pointing up, ears flopping down.
Short tails, long tails, brown stripes white.
Too many cheeky dogs.
Too many fights.

Shhhh . . . time for the dogs to go to sleep.

NORTH SOUTH EAST WEST
I LOVE
HOME BEST
TENNANT CREEK

I fly again to visit my friends.
Kristie and Brad.
Kristie was in Tennant Creek before.
She showed me how to talk with my hands.

Hello. How are you? Beautiful! Thanks.
Don't talk about that little white dog!
Running. Fighting. Lost in the grass.
You were crying, crying.
Everyone was sad looking for that dog.
Oh, there he is! Quickly, quickly put him somewhere safe.

Now Kristie lives in Hervey Bay.
We go out looking for whales.
Enormous tails above our tiny boat.
Flipping and flopping.
A bit like me in the pool at Tennant Creek.

whale
sea
Dion
W

I splash around and twist and turn.
The water holds me up.

Joie playing. Pushing me down.
My bum hitting the tiles.
Again. Please do it again!

Black beetles in the lane ropes hide
and water skippers too.
After the rain a blanket of grasshoppers.
Green ones. Yellow ones.
Big brown spotty ones.
The lifeguards try to scoop them up
but more keep coming.

I try to go swimming every day.
Last year they closed the pool.

NO SWIMMING ALLOWED!

Lots of men and diggers and piles of dirt.
Can I swim? Can I swim?
No, not yet.
When the pool reopens
I'm the first one there.

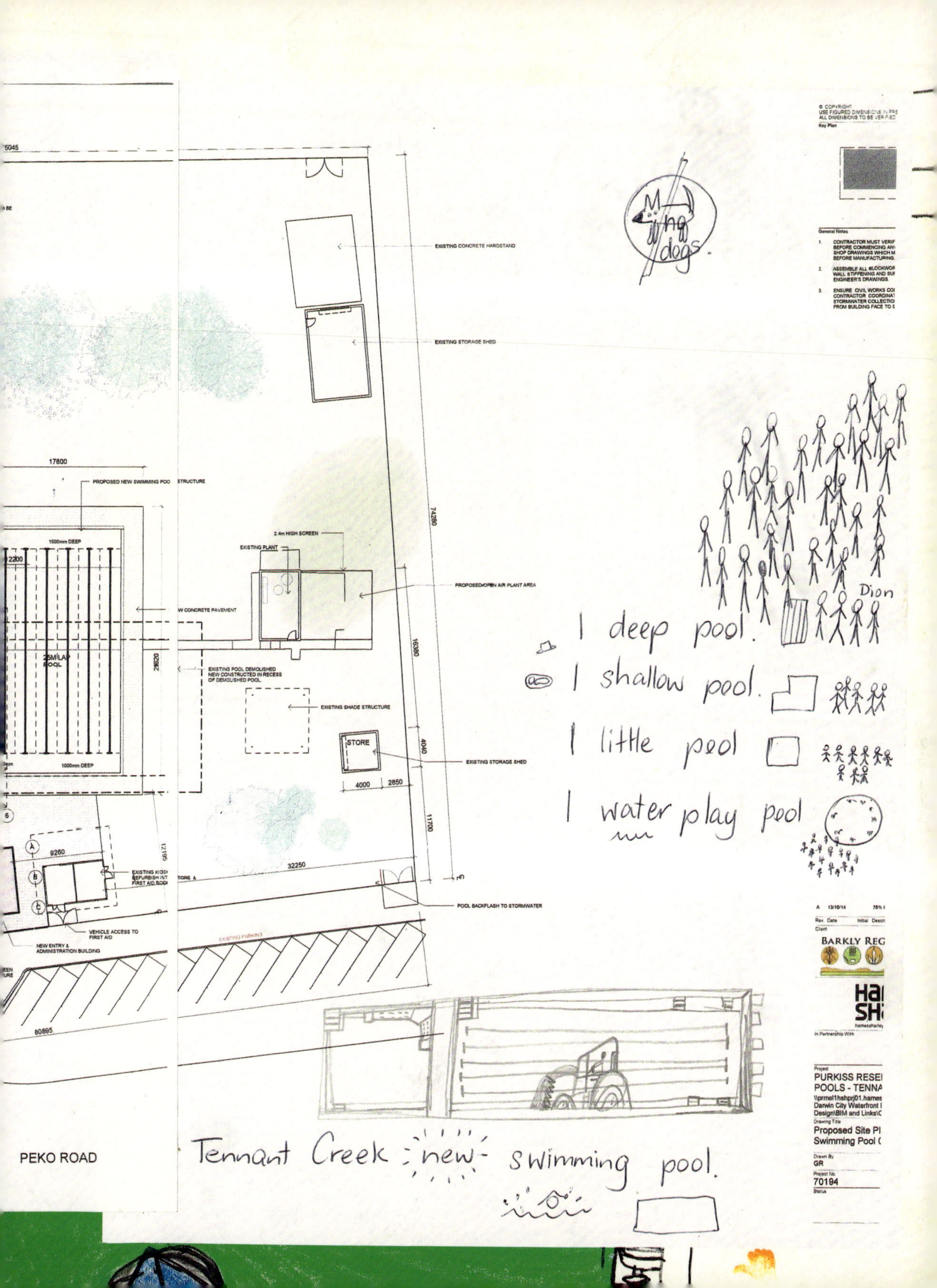

no dogs
Dion
1 deep pool.
1 shallow pool.
1 little pool
1 water play pool
Tennant Creek new swimming pool.
PEKO ROAD
EXISTING CONCRETE HARDSTAND
EXISTING STORAGE SHED
PROPOSED NEW SWIMMING POOL STRUCTURE
2.4m HIGH SCREEN
EXISTING PLANT
PROPOSED OPEN AIR PLANT AREA
1500mm DEEP
25M LAP POOL
1000mm DEEP
EXISTING POOL DEMOLISHED NEW CONSTRUCTED IN RECESS OF DEMOLISHED POOL.
EXISTING SHADE STRUCTURE
STORE
POOL BACKFLASH TO STORMWATER
VEHICLE ACCESS TO FIRST AID
NEW ENTRY & ADMINISTRATION BUILDING
EXISTING PARKING
BARKLY REG
PURKISS RESEI
POOLS - TENNA
Proposed Site Pl
Swimming Pool (
70194

no
dogs.

At Lake Nash there are two rivers.
Big ones – Rankin and Georgina.
Lots of small ones too like snakes running into the lake.

When I was little
four maybe five
it rained and rained
and it didn't stop.
The rivers grew big.
The snakes disappeared.
The sky was on the ground
clouds in the lake.
The water coming up, up, up.

My dad was there.

He picked me up.

Strong arms

and carried me across.

We got stuck in a river once, me, Tony and Joie.
Tony was driving the big white car.
Don't cross the river Joie said.
But Tony had a different idea.
Too deep! Too deep!
Car lifting up, spinning around.

Water coming in up to our feet
our legs, our waists!
Me floating, floating.
Joie swimming out, holding onto the bull bar.
Seatbelt off, Joie pulling me out.
Water, water everywhere. Mud on my feet.
We were very lucky Joie said.
Tony wasn't. He lost his thong.

We fight sometimes, Tony and me.
I like playing tricks that make him cross.
When he's asleep I wheel into his room
quiet, quiet
and switch on all the lights!
Tony makes big eyes. He has to get out of bed.
Me gone by then, laughing, laughing.

I play other tricks too.
I turn my fingers into dogs at the dinner table.
Backwards and forwards they run
knocking over plates and spilling the ginger beer.
BURP!
Don't you be doing that Tony says.

I hide Tony's favourite saltshaker
and the eye drops he got from the doctor.
Sometimes I pull the toilet roll off
and turn it into a road.
All the way to Lake Nash.
Rough, rough, bumpy, bumpy.
Seven hours from here, it takes
and you can only go
after the big rains stop.

Tony

One day, I'm going back to Lake Nash
with Angela and Damilia.
Her eyes don't work and I can't hear.
We're a funny bunch Joie says.
I want to take my scooter but I need
a special trailer for that.
Tony will make me one he says.
And Angela will pull it over the bumps.
Rough, rough, bumpy, bumpy
all the way back to my family
in Lake Nash.

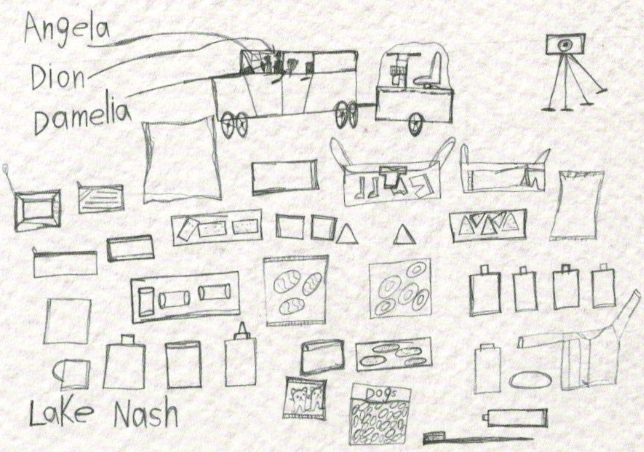

Dion

J
Jonathon
Kaylene
April
Rod
Gloria
Eric
Warric
Sean
Rosella
Rowan
Mason

sharon
Harold
Elizabeth
ntaisha
Don
Sheronah
Dalvin
Johnny

Dreaming I am
always dreaming
of monsters that come
in the night.
Three blind boys
walking past my room.
A blue man taller than
the moon.
The giant dog that
lives at the dump.
Look out!
He can squash you
with one foot.
Quick Joie.
Close the window!
Close the door!
And turn on all
the lights!

no

Ø
Ø no
Ø no
no
Ø no
Ø no
Ø no
Ø no
Ø no
Ø no
Ø no
Ø no
no
Ø no
Ø no
Ø no
Ø no
Ø no
Ø no
Ø no
Ø no
Ø no
Ø no
Ø no
Ø no
Ø no
Ø no
Ø no
Ø no
Ø no
Ø

Scared too of frogs in the shower
their black eyes staring out.
Looking, looking, ready to jump.

Quick Joie! Get the plastic lids
and cover all the holes.

Dreaming too of a room where the sun never leaves.
Sun on the window, sun across my bed.
Joie puts mirrors outside my room to catch the light
but still night comes.

I tell Brett to build me
a house out the back.
Brett is Joie's brother's son.
My cousin. Sort of.
With my hands I tell him
My new house must have
one room full of sunshine
and a bath tub.
There's no bath
at Fazaldeen Road.

Dreaming too of going overseas to Africa.
Who will come? Joie? No. Tony? No.
Who then? I don't know yet.
But I will go with someone young.
We will be looking out the window
for animals running very fast.

Dion

Elephants
rhinos
tall giraffes
buffalo
zebras
wildebeest.
Even
a hippopotamus
but no dogs.

NO DOGS ALLOWED!

Going on safari, me in the back.
Quick! Lock the window.
Check it. Check it again.
Don't go opening the window Joie says
Or the lion will jump in and swallow you.

Dion

I talk with my hands signing, signing.

Wendy taught me first
and Anna and my friend Kristie
and Dan the policeman too.
If we can't find a sign
we just make it up.

Dog
two pats on the leg
Fox
sign for F + sign for snout
Wolf
sign for W + sign for snout
Hyena
sign for H + sign for snout
African hunting dog
sign for wild + sign for dog

And don't get us started on cats.

EOS 70D
Canon
Canon

Every morning **Is it time yet?**
Nearly Joie says.
Out of the freezer comes the meat.
Bones and sausages and chicken necks.
Butcher knife on the bricks, me chopping up.
Be careful! Or you'll cut your finger off.
We can't have that Joie says.

Meat in my bag and dog biscuits too.
Backing out and full throttle go!
Down the driveway I zoom.
At the main road, turn left.
Whizz past the school, old ladies on the grass.
Their skirts bright and legs crossed.
They give me a nod.

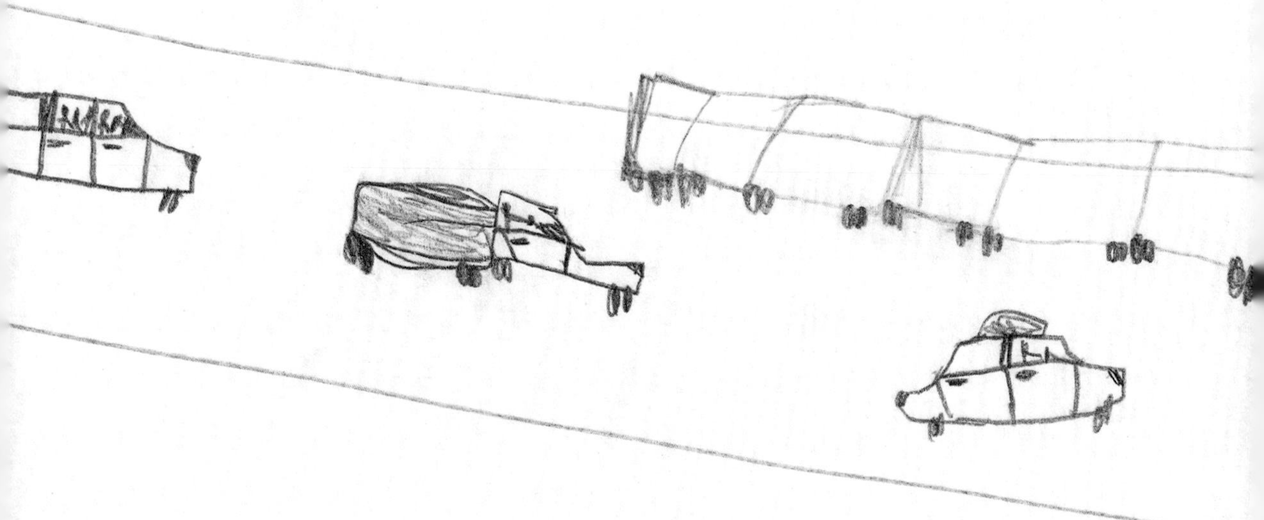

Playing chicken on the footpath with the kids.
Who will move first? Not me!
They duck away and high five as I pass.

Past the police station where Dan used to work.
Slowly, slowly. Quiet, quiet.
At Peko Road, I go to cross.
STOP! WAIT!
Don't go getting squashed by a road train Joie says.
Slowly nudging out.
Waving to the cars passing by.
Sometimes they wave back.
Past the bus shelter near the park
and the Goldfields Hotel and the newsagency.
Past Wyatt Motors with the big high fence.
Two black dogs come charging out.
Sharp teeth. Jumping up.
Barking, barking, but I'm too fast.
Fast like a cheetah not slow like a turtle.

No dogs!
Where are they?

It's too hot says Joie.

They're all asleep.

I'll come back when the sun goes down.

Then all the dogs come running.
Big ones. Small ones.
Black brown white.
Dogs with spots and dogs with stripes.

The food is gone and the clouds are fat.
Dark ones with the rain coming out.
Hurry, hurry! Faster, faster!
Must get home before the water comes up.
Don't get stuck! Who will carry me across?

Car coming, car coming.
Straight at me.
Get off the road Joie says.

NEVER. EVER.
DO. THAT.
AGAIN.
YOU. SILLY. BOY.

Gave me a fright she says. ***I get worried.***
But next day she lets me go again.
She knows I am happy
feeding the dogs at Mulga Camp.

Once, I rode my scooter up to the tip.
In and out of the gutter I went.
In out, in out. Wheels shaking.
Uh-oh! Wheels stuck.
I waited but nobody came.
It got dark.
I left my scooter
and crawled back to the house.
Home again. Home again.
My hands and knees were sore from all the rocks.

Every year the show comes to Tennant Creek.
Big rides going dizzy fast.
Flipping, dipping, whizzing past.
Dizzy chairs. Motorbikes.
Sideways shaker. Cage of Death.

BOYS WITH LEGS
THAT DON'T WORK
AREN'T ALLOWED.

That's what the man who sells the tickets says.

I go on the dodgems instead.

Cars bouncing this way and that.
Zipping, racing, bumping, biting.
Just like the dogs at Mulga Camp.
Fighting, fighting, always fighting.
No crashing allowed! says Joie.
But I look the other way so I can't see her hands.
Bang, bang, crash, crash.
My hat flies off.
I watch it get squashed
and I smile.

My friend Dan gets me onto all the rides.
At Dreamworld and Sea World and
Wet 'n' Wild slide world.
Bumping sideways
upside down.
Swirling twisting
spinning round.
My eyes are big like tractor tyres.
Faster, faster, faster we go.
Like the dogs at Mulga Camp.
Like the river at Lake Nash
after the rain.

I want to stay on all day long but Dan says no.
Time to go home.

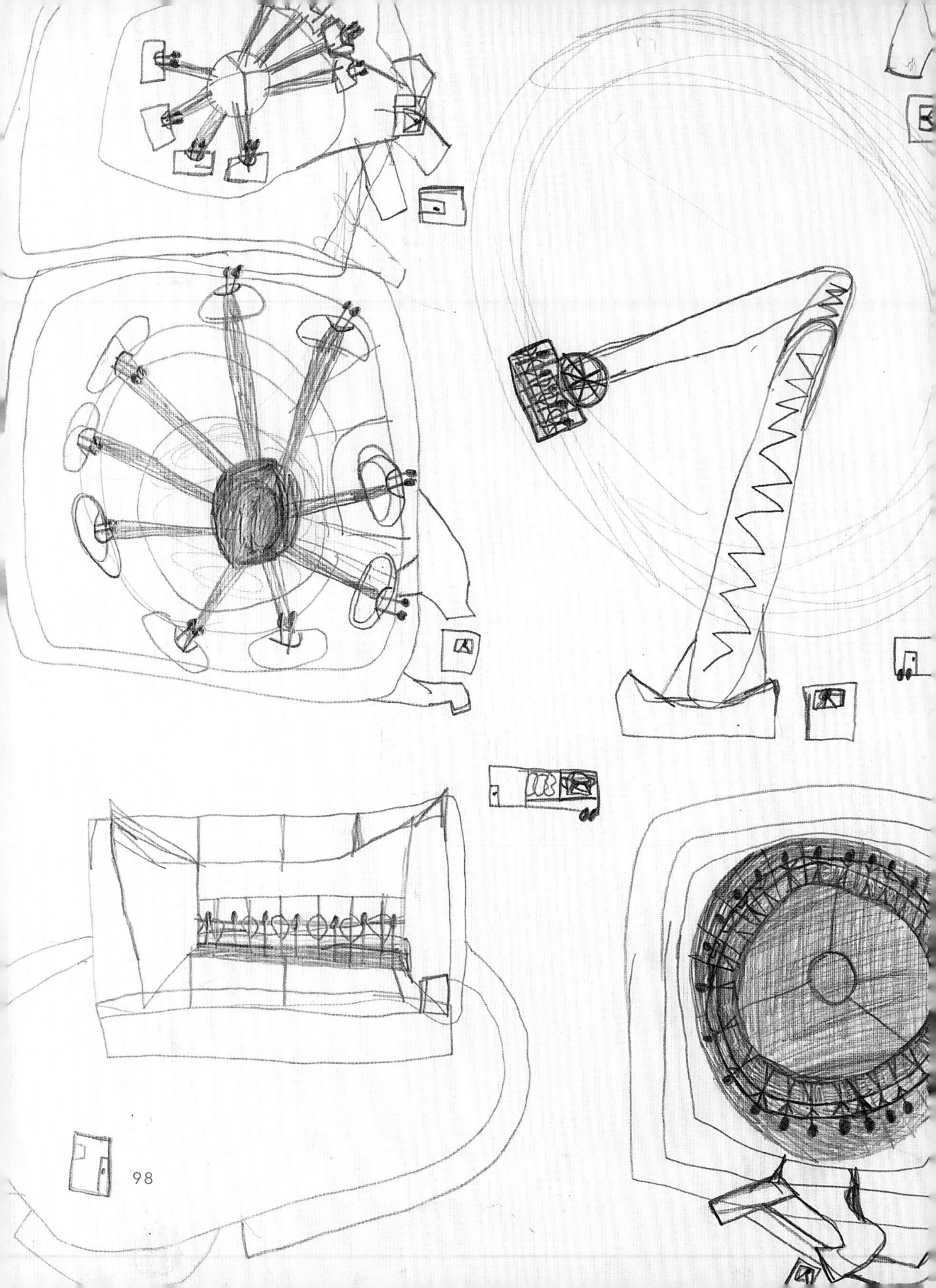

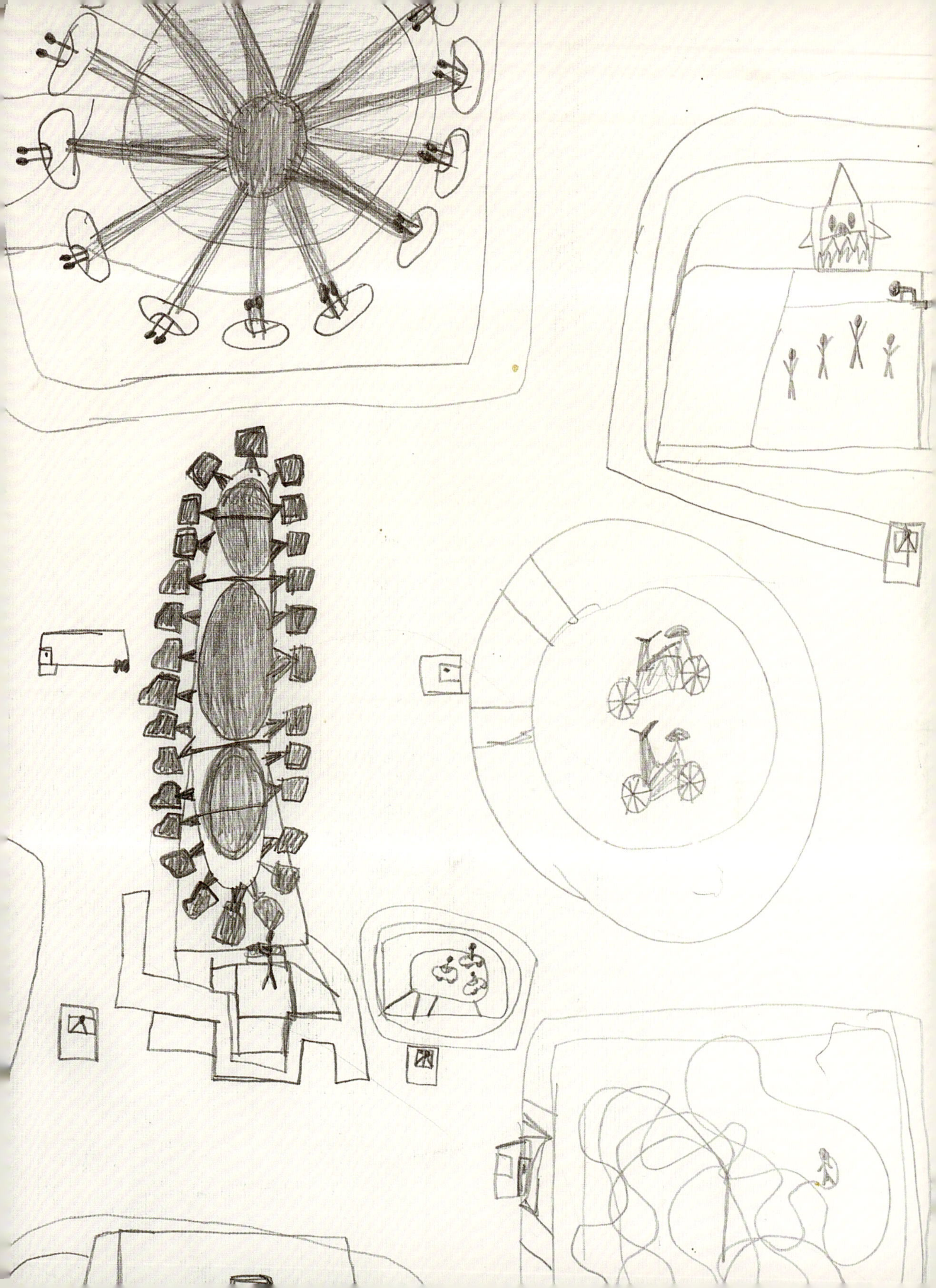

Last year my tooth was
sore, crying in the night.
Joie took me to Alice
Springs to get it pulled out.
Gas mask, dizzy head.
Room spinning around,
then falling asleep.
I dreamed about a bee.
Big wings. Stretching out.
Stung me on the finger once,
my body blowing up.
Bigger and bigger,
same as a balloon.
STOP! It might pop.
Then I woke up and my
tooth was gone.

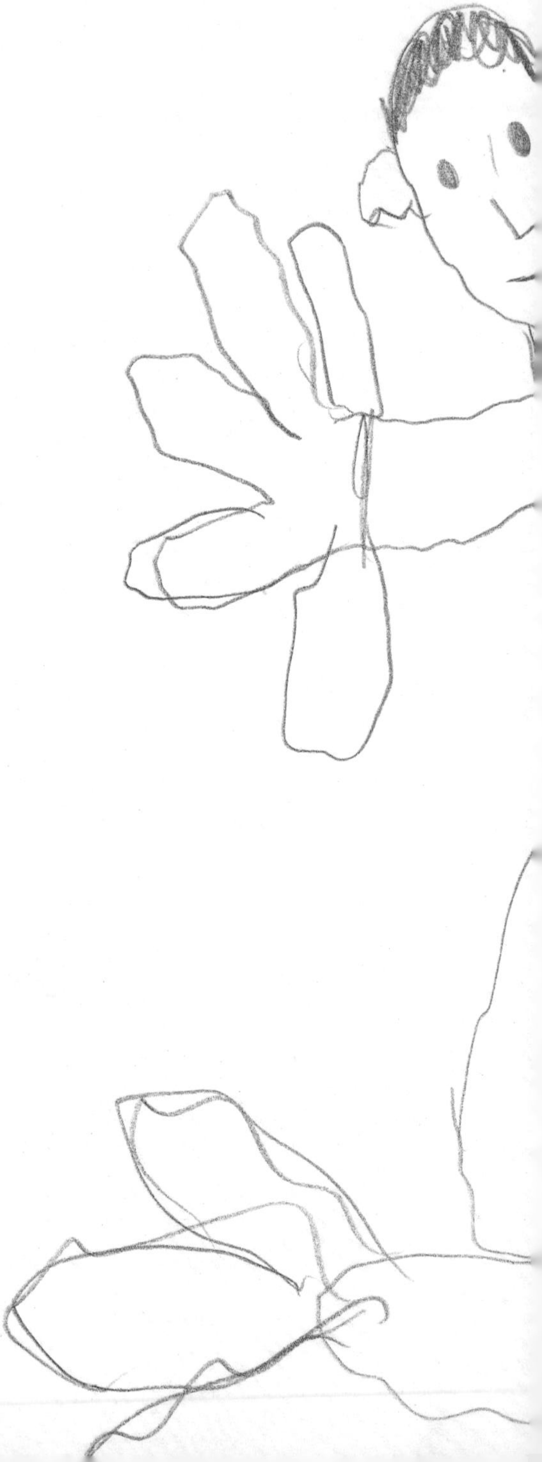

My mum is gone.
They buried her in Lake Nash under the ground.
We drive out there in the big white car.
Red earth. Grey fence.
We take flowers from the store, plastic ones.
Green. Pink. Yellow. Red.
They look small against the dirt.

My grandmother is sorry.
I am sorry too.
My mother is gone.
Her bones stay in the ground but the meat falls off.
That's what I tell Joie.

I sad boy crying

6

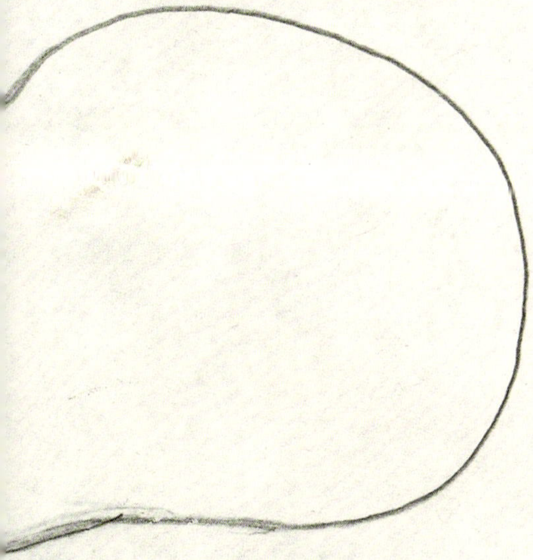

When my grandad died
everyone stopped me in the street.
They were shaking my hand.

I'm sorry they said.

I was sorry too.
I went down to number six
but Grandad wasn't sitting
at the table.

I think a lot about the little white dog.
The one Joie dropped in the grass near the show.
Don't. You. Be. Talking. About. That! says Joie.
But I do. I keep saying it.
I like to see her hop around, flapping her arms like a brolga bird.
She looks cross but really she's not.

Joie is next to me. I'm drawing, drawing.
Beautiful! she says.
My hand is on her arm, in her hair, pulling, pulling.
Letting Joie know she's my best.

Except when I'm cross, she's not.
I draw her dead in the ground with Tony too and everybody crying.
Dan the policeman. Kristie in Hervey Bay,
Johanna with the curly hair, Joie's family in Victoria
and all the old ladies down at Mulga Camp.
Crying, crying, crying.

One day Joie will be gone.
Her meat will fall off.
Where will I live?
Who will make me sausages and chips?
Who will stop the frogs jumping out?
Who will keep the light on in the middle of the night?
And who will say my drawings are beautiful?

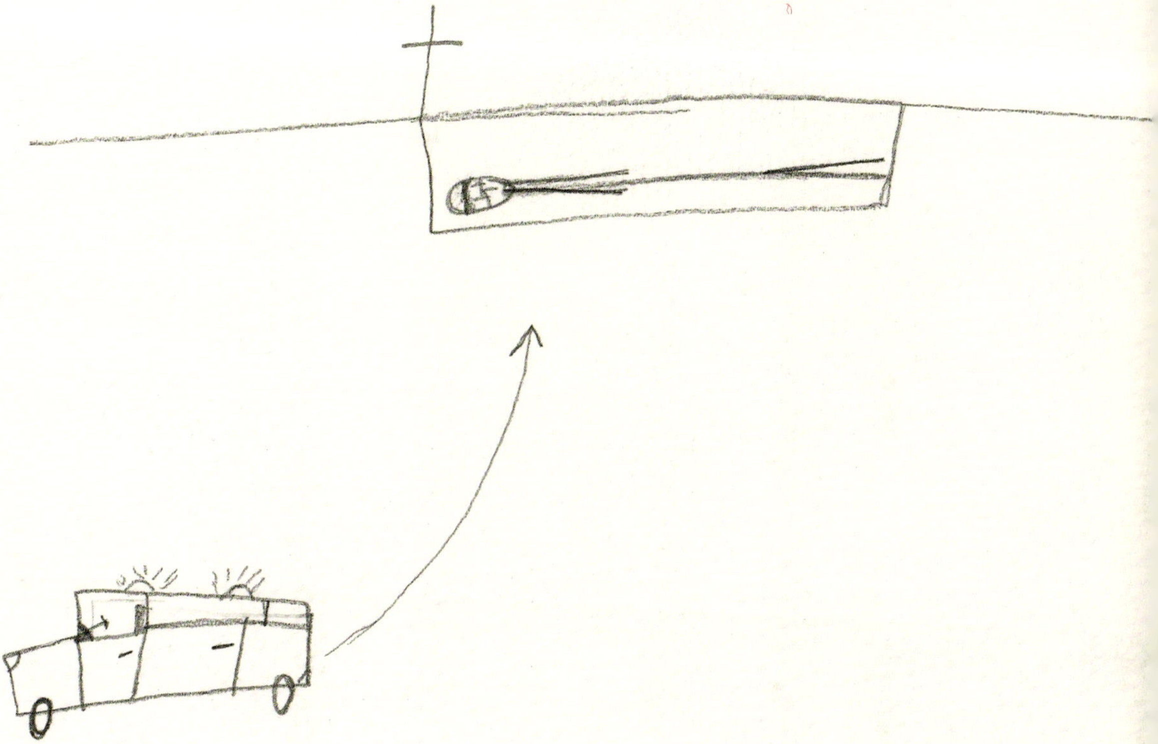

The Lion King is dead and
Tony's grey cat and
Trouble and Bessie and
my mother and my grandad and
all the old dogs from Mulga Camp
Who will be next? I think.

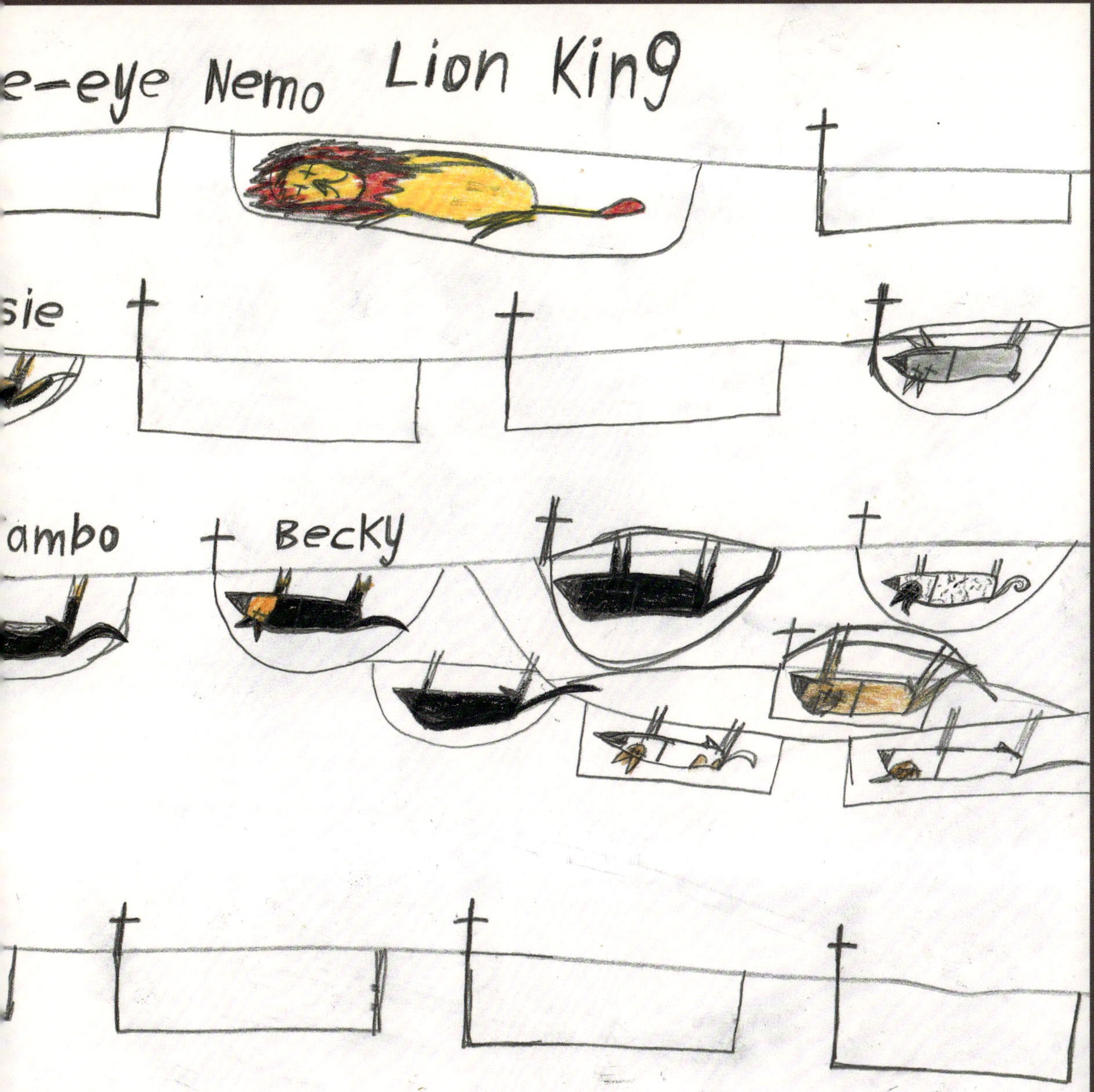
e-eye Nemo
Lion King
sie
ambo
Becky

I look up and see the black clouds coming.
Quickly! Quickly! Don't get stuck!
Back door open, just a crack
so I can watch the first drops hit the pavement.
Round like my eyes opening up.
Soon everything is wet.
Water, water, everywhere.
Quick Joie! Close the door!

I was scared
when I was small
four, maybe five.
Walking to the shop.
Three angry grey dogs.
Hair up. Sharp teeth.
Me on the ground.
Their teeth in my skin.

A man was there, picking me up.

What would have happened if he was not?

This year, I'll be going back.
Rough, rough, bumpy, bumpy.
All the way to Lake Nash.

Past the place with no trees. Completely flat.
Past the little rivers like snakes sliding into the lake.
More than seven hours on a bumpy road
dust flying out the back.

To the brown house where we used to live.
Mum, Dad, my sister and me.
Making damper, cooking kangaroo.

Swimming down near the bridge with the kids.
Splashing. Laughing. Slapping the water.

Watching the dogs.
Black dogs brown dogs white dogs red.
Mothers, brothers, father dogs.
One eye open. One ear up.
Always only half asleep.

Riding on my scooter to the shop for a drink.
Cold one – orange, lemon, red.
The dogs will be there.
Big ones with sharp teeth.
Hair up, ready to fight.
I remember teeth in my skin.
I feel the scar on my stomach, long and thin.

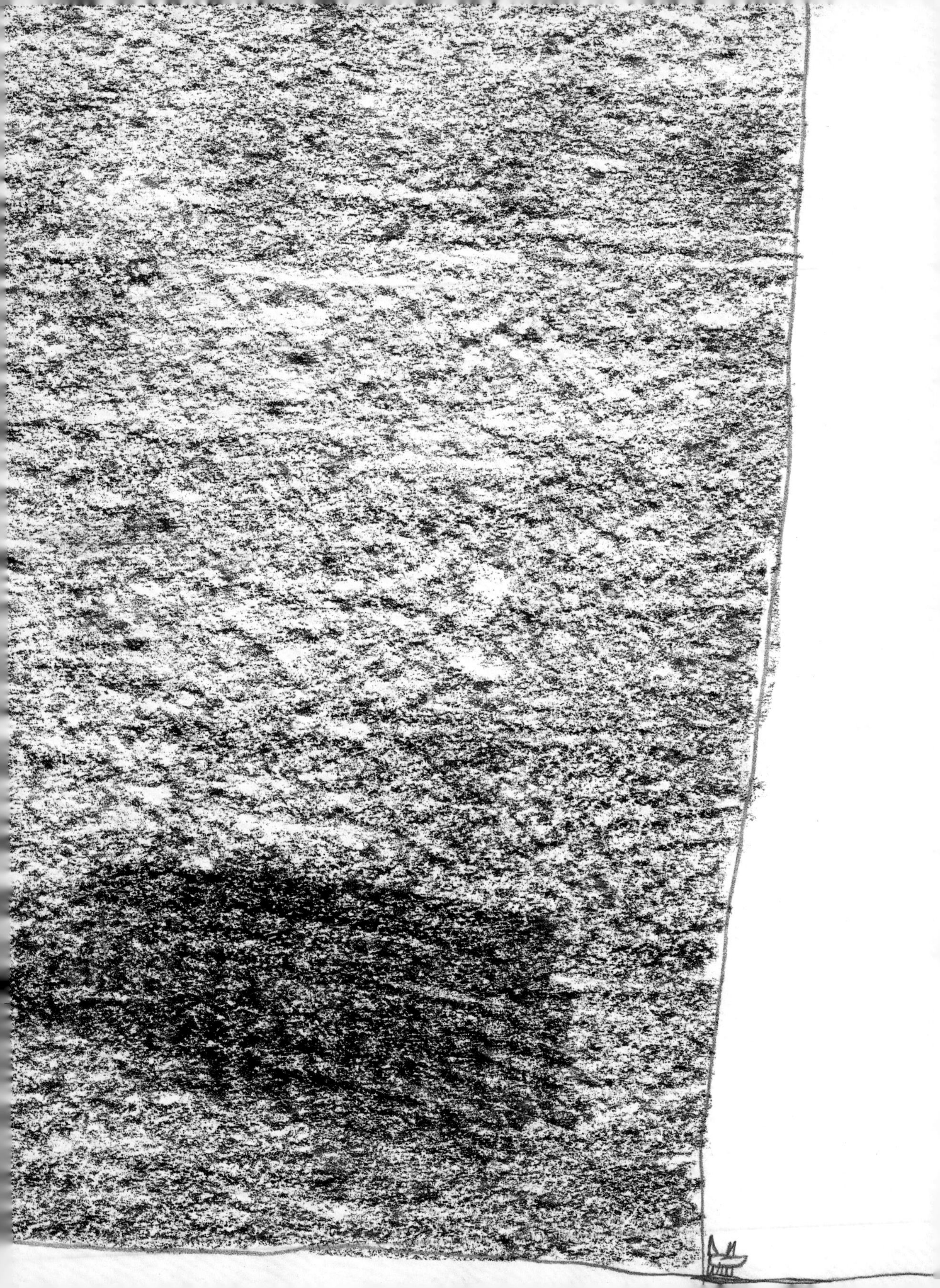

No! Not this time!
I'm big now and strong.
They can't get me.

I buy my fizzy orange drink.
Stop and wait.
Family in the shade, dogs at my feet.
Opening it. Cold can on my lips.
Down, down, down it goes.
Eyes closed, waiting for the air rushing up.
Rumbling, rumbling, stomach then throat.
BURP!
Everybody looks.
Mothers. Fathers. Brothers. Cousins.
Even the dogs.
Everybody.
Laughing, laughing.
It feels good to be home again
with family
in Lake Nash.

113
112

1
2
3
4
5
6
7
8
9
10
11
12
13
14
15
16
17
18

The Story Behind the Story

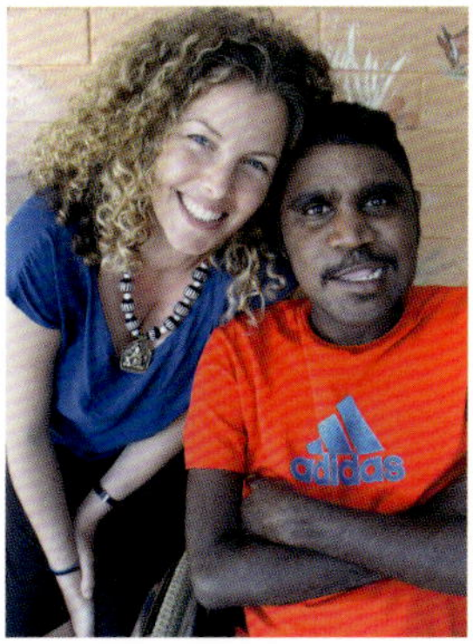

For **DION BEASLEY**, who has muscular dystrophy and profound deafness, drawing is one way he expresses observations, ideas, dreams and childhood memories. He loves creating works that feature Lake Nash (his mother's country), Canteen Creek (his father's country), Mulga Camp (where his grandfather lived) and the antics of Tennant Creek's many camp dogs.

When Dion was eleven, he moved to Tennant Creek to live with his grandfather. With no speech and limited Auslan, Dion found primary school tough. Joie Boulter, one of the teaching staff (and now Dion's carer and guardian) noticed how much he loved to draw camp dogs. She bought him a stack of paper and pencils and encouraged his art. Dion drew every day and in 2006, Joie helped him establish his own textile company, Cheeky Dogs, which has become a much-loved Northern Territory brand. Around the same time, Dion's drawings caught the attention of the fine arts world, leading to solo exhibitions, collaborations, acquisitions, and an invitation to exhibit at the Museum of Contemporary Art in Sydney.

Meanwhile, almost 1000km north of Tennant Creek, **JOHANNA BELL**, a social researcher and aspiring children's author, was hatching a plan. After working in remote preschools across the Northern Territory, she realised that there weren't enough children's books about the lived experiences of remote Indigenous children. Determined to create a book to support remote literacy, Johanna was drawn to Dion's humorous drawings of camp dogs. She phoned Joie and asked if Dion might be interested, to which Joie replied, 'Why don't you pop down to Tennant Creek and we can see how it goes?'

Two years, three grants, several light aircraft flights, a crash course in Auslan and lots of laughs later, *Too Many Cheeky Dogs* hit the bookstores.

In 2017, Johanna and Dion's second book *Go Home Cheeky Animals!* won the CBCA Book of the Year (early childhood). *Cheeky Dogs: To Lake Nash and Back* is their third book together.

Facing page: Dion's storyboard for this book.

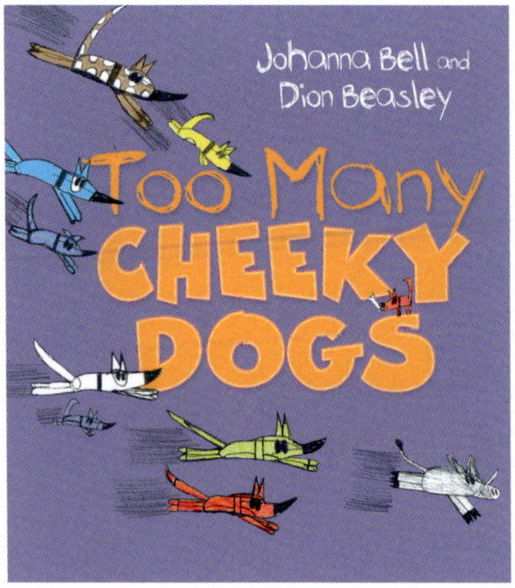

SHORTLISTED REAL Awards, Picture Storybook

SHORTLISTED Territory Read Awards, Children's and YA

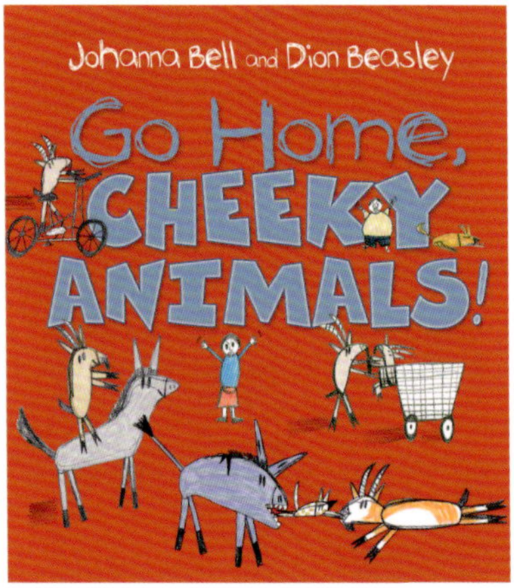

WINNER CBCA Book of the Year, Early Childhood

WINNER Territory Read Book of the Year, Children's and YA

SHORTLISTED Speech Pathology Australia Book of the Year – Indigenous Children

Photo Credits

Page 24 Johanna Bell; pages 42–3, pages 44–5 Lincoln MacKinnon, Barkly Regional Arts; page 47 owned by Joie Boulter (let us know if you took this photo!); page 84–5 Lincoln MacKinnon, Barkly Regional Arts; pages 94–5 Johanna Bell; page 121 Ruth Grüner.

Acknowledgements

Dion's memoir was made possible by the enthusiasm and generosity of many. Biggest thanks to Joie Boulter, who made sure Dion's voice was ever-present and fed us endless pancakes. Thanks to our publishing team at Allen & Unwin, especially Erica Wagner, Matariki Williams and Kate Whitfield. We're so grateful for your ideas and your commitment to tell unconventional stories. A special thanks to Ruth Grüner for agreeing to work with us again (even though she knows we're hard work). Your impeccable design skills transformed our work beyond what we'd imagined possible. Thanks to Barkly Regional Arts for sharing their photographic collection and to Lincoln MacKenzie for taking such wonderful photos. A special thanks to Dion's family, past and present, for helping Dion share his stories. Thanks to all Dion's friends who appear in this book – Tony, Dan, Kristie, Brad, Anna, Angela, Damilia and Brett, and to Joie's family for their ongoing support. Thanks too to Oscar Schwartz for editorial feedback and to Courtney Collins, Jess Ong, Clare Atkins and Mary Anne Butler for being wonderful wing women. Thanks to Grace Heifetz for all the books to come and to Jano Gibson for helping generate the space needed to tell this story.